Desert Morsels

A JOURNAL

*with Encouraging Tidbits
from My Journey on the
Weigh Down™ Diet*

Jan Christiansen

STARBURST PUBLISHERS®

P. O. Box 4123, Lancaster, Pennsylvania 17604

To schedule author appearances, write:

Author Appearances
Starburst Promotions
P.O. Box 4123
Lancaster, Pennsylvania 17604

or call (717) 293-0939

www.starburstpublishers.com

First Printing, January, 2000
ISBN: 1-892016-214
Library of Congress Catalog Number 99-67258
Printed in the United States of America

Cover design by Richmond & Williams
Text design and composition by John Reinhardt Book Design

You know that feeling you get when you are hungry and want something good to eat, but don't know what it is? You know it has to be something tasty, something that will really hit the spot, but you can't put your finger on just what it is that will satisfy the craving. Rummaging around in the pantry you consider different foods, but can't find that tasty morsel you are looking for, so you turn to the fridge, but it's not there either.

My friend, you are looking in all the wrong places! Let me give you a hint . . . it's smaller than a breadbox and contains the bread of life. That's right—you will find what you are looking for in the Bible!

As I make my way through the desert to the Promised Land of thinness, I keep finding these tiny tidbits of spiritual nourishment in God's word. They have been a great source of strength and encouragement to me as I learn to submit my eating habits to God. It's these choice morsels of scripture that have helped me to stay on the right path and progress steadily toward my goal.

Desert Morsels is a veritable feast of motivational appetizers, spread for you like a banquet in the desert. Help yourself to whatever you like. Fill your plate. You don't have to worry about calories or fat grams in these juicy treats, because they have been prepared by the Divine Chef to satisfy your deepest hunger and thirst. Please feel free to return to the table and refill your plate as many times as you wish, because this is an "All You Can Eat Buffet" that never closes.

I've included plenty of room on each page for you to jot down your thoughts or your own Desert Morsels as you find them. I've thrown in some real gourmet treats called P-attitudes (not to be confused with Beatitudes).

I've even sprinkled in a few testimonies from my desert buddies who frequent Jan's Journals, my internet web site (www.ohiowebsites.com). Their stories are sure to inspire and motivate you as you read about their success at losing weight.

So, you're all set! Pick a few morsels and pack them in your picnic basket as you head out through the sand dunes. When the going gets tough and you're beginning to feel a bit parched, find yourself a shady place to sit and chew on these Desert Morsels a while. I'm sure they will fortify you for the next leg of your journey.

Happy traveling!
Jan

1

P-Attitudes

ATTITUDES

P-ATTITUDES ARE THOSE ATTITUDES WHICH CAN HELP OR HINDER US ON OUR JOURNEY. I'VE PLACED THESE THROUGHOUT THE BOOK TO POINT OUT THOSE WHICH HAVE THE POTENTIAL OF MAKING OUR TIME IN THE DESERT A PLEA-SURE AS WELL AS A FEW THAT COULD BE POS-SIBLE PITFALLS. WATCH OUT FOR THE P-ATTITUDES!

"Therefore I am now going to allure her;
I will lead her into the desert and speak tenderly to her . . ."

HOSEA 2:14

What a wonderful picture of God's love for you! And you thought it was *your* decision to begin this desert journey . . . you were wrong. God, Himself has been wooing you, gently alluring you into the desert. He wants you to succeed!

_____

_____

_____

_____

_____

_____

P-Attitudes

PRAISE

Praise God in the desert. Praise Him for every small achievement, praise Him for lessons learned in the setbacks and praise Him in advance for the final victory. But most of all praise Him for who He is— the Almighty Creator of heaven and earth!

PSALM 147:1

"This only have I found: God made mankind upright, but men have gone in search of many schemes."

ECCLESIASTES 7:29

God designed our bodies to operate perfectly—to maintain our normal weight. We short-circuited that mechanism by overeating, and we have gone in search of many schemes to solve the problem. Let's forget the schemes and return to God's plan for eating.

_____

_____

_____

_____

_____

_____

P-Attitudes

PRAYER

OPEN COMMUNICATION WITH THE FATHER AS
YOU TRAVEL ALLOWS HIM TO KEEP YOU ON
THE RIGHT PATH. PRAYER IS THE PROPELLANT
THAT FUELS YOU TOWARD THE PROMISED LAND.

COLOSSIANS 4:2

Blessed is He whose transgressions are forgiven, whose sins are covered. Blessed is the man whose sin the LORD does not count against Him and in whose spirit is no deceit.

PSALM 32:1–2

*D*id you ask God to forgive you for overeating? Then rejoice—you may now live guilt-free! Your transgressions are forgiven, your sins are covered and the Lord does not count it against you anymore!

_____

_____

_____

_____

_____

_____

_____

P-Attitudes

PROMISE

GOD'S WORD IS TRUE. EVERY PROMISE HE HAS MADE, HE WILL DO. PICK UP HIS WORD DAILY AND READ THE PROMISES HE HAS MADE TO YOU—HIS CHILD. HIDE THEM IN YOUR HEART WITH THE FULL ASSURANCE THAT THEY WILL COME TO PASS.

JAMES 1:12

Nehemiah said, "Go and enjoy choice food and sweet drinks, and send some to those who have nothing prepared. This day is sacred to our LORD. Do not grieve, for the joy of the LORD is your strength."

NEHEMIAH 8:10

There is great joy in knowing that we can enjoy all the yummy foods God placed here on earth—choice food and sweet drink. So, enjoy your food today, but only between the parameters of hungry and satisfied!

_____

_____

_____

_____

_____

_____

_____   _____

*Being confident of this, that he who began a good work
in you will carry it on to completion
until the day of Christ Jesus.*

PHILIPPIANS 1:6

You can be confident that this time you will lose weight! God has begun His good work in you . . . the good work of conforming you into the image of His Son, Jesus Christ, and you can be sure that He will continue to do that until the day Jesus returns.

Many of us approach losing weight with some anxiety because we have tried so many times in the past and failed. Don't worry, this time you won't fail because you are not going on a diet, you are going on a live it! You will be learning how to live each day within God's will where your eating is concerned. He will be teaching you how to read your body's signals for true hunger and satisfaction and He will direct you in making wise food choices so that your body can operate at peak performance.

Bit by bit, you will be changed in body and in spirit until you conform to the image of Christ. He was, after all, completely obedient to the Father's will, wasn't He? Will you be perfect? Probably not (make that definitely not), but if you will be consistent in your desire to please Him, you will realize your goals and achieve your normal weight.

So hold your head high, my friend—let your confidence in God soar as you realize that this time you will make it. He will not give up on you even when you *blow it*, and He won't let up on you even when you try to squirm out of obedience.

He has begun His good work in you and He is determined to shape you in the image of His Son, so hang on . . . you're going for the ride of your life and you are going to love it!

PS: Look over your shoulder . . . I'm right there with you. I still need a bit of shaping myself!

All man's efforts are for his mouth,
yet his appetite is never satisfied.

ECCLESIASTES 6:7

If all your efforts are for your mouth, your appetite will never be satisfied, but if all your efforts are for the Lord, you will know no end to satisfaction. Take your pick!

P-Attitudes

PASSION

Be passionate about your relationship with God! Let your emotions be stirred as you think of His love for you and that you are His cherished bride. Think of this desert journey as your honeymoon with your Heavenly Husband!

JEREMIAH 31:3

*There is not a righteous man on earth
who does what is right and never sins.*

ECCLESIASTES 7:20

id you blow it? Don't worry about it. God was not surprised. He knows that there is not one righteous man on earth who does what is right and never sins. That's why He sent Jesus—repent and start again!

_____

_____

_____

_____

_____

_____

P-Attitudes

POTENTIAL

GOD HAS PLANTED MORE POTENTIAL INSIDE YOU THAN YOU COULD EVER IMAGINE. TAP INTO THAT POTENTIALITY AND DARE TO STEP OUT, STEP UP, AND STEP OVER! BE ALL THAT HE HAS DESIGNED YOU TO BE.

EPHESIANS 2:10

As no one is discharged in time of war,
so wickedness will not release those who practice it.

ECCLESIASTES 8:8B

Soldiers are not discharged in time of war and sin will not release those who practice it. If you want to be free from the battle of sinful overeating, you will have to go AWOL!

_____

_____

_____

_____

_____

_____

P-Attitudes

POWER

FORGET ABOUT *WILLPOWER*! INSTEAD, MAKE
USE OF GOD'S POWER TO TEACH YOU TO SAY
"NO" TO UNGODLINESS AND WORLDLY DESIRES
AND HOW TO LIVE SELF-DISCIPLINED, UPRIGHT,
AND GODLY LIVES.

TITUS 2:11

Jesus replied, "If anyone loves me, he will obey my teaching. My Father will love him, and we will come to him and make our home with him. He who does not love me will not obey my teaching. . . ."

JOHN 14:23–24A

If you love Him, you will obey Him. If you are not walking in obedience, perhaps you had better examine just how much you love Him.

_____

_____

_____

_____

_____

_____

"I am the true vine, and my Father is the gardener. He cuts off every branch in me that bears no fruit, while every branch that does bear fruit he prunes so that it will be even more fruitful."

John 15:1–2

I'm being pruned . . . I can feel it.

Have you ever been to Disneyland? The grounds are meticulously groomed. The shrubs are shaped and cared for as they grow so that when they reach maturity, they are in the image of an animal or a Disney character.

That's what's happening to me—God is shaping me and pruning me! Sometimes it feels good to have the dead bark and wilting leaves stripped away, and sometimes it hurts like crazy to have the Master Gardener cut away branches that I am not yet ready to let go of. But I know that each snip of the pruning shears serves only to make me stronger in the end, for I am being groomed in the image of Jesus Christ, so that I will bear much fruit for Him.

I want to bear fruit in my life. I want people to look at me . . . look at the fruit of my life and say, "We can tell by the fruit that she is a branch who is fully connected to the True Vine." So while the pruning process is not always pleasant, I will yield myself to His care. How about you?

When I tried to understand all this, it was oppressive to me
till I entered the sanctuary of God;
then I understood their final destiny.

PSALM 73:16–17

Diets, calories, fat grams, proteins, carbohydrates, cholesterol . . . when I tried to understand all this, it was oppressive to me till I entered the sanctuary of God—trusting Him to teach me the proper way to eat.

P-Attitudes

PLAYING

PLAYING WITH DISOBEDIENCE IS A DANGEROUS PASTIME, CERTAIN TO LEAD YOU INTO DEFEAT. IT'S LIKE ONE OF THOSE TOYS THAT NEED TO BE RECALLED BECAUSE OF ITS POTENTIAL TO HARM A CHILD. REMEMBER THAT YOU ARE GOD'S CHILD, SO BE CAREFUL WHAT YOU PLAY WITH!

HEBREWS 4:6

The LORD abhors dishonest scales,
but accurate weights are his delight.

PROVERBS 11:1

Don't let the scales stress you out. They are inaccurate measures for what the Lord is doing in your life. They cannot weigh the value of an obedient spirit!

_____

_____

_____

_____

_____

_____

P-Attitudes

PITY

PLOPPING DOWN ON A SAND DUNE TO HAVE A PITY PARTY FOR YOURSELF WILL ONLY PRO-LONG YOUR JOURNEY AND LEAVE YOU WITH SAND IN YOUR SHORTS. GET UP, SHAKE OUT THE SAND, AND GET MOVING. LEAVE THE SELF-PITY BURIED IN THE SAND.

PSALM 68:3

My heart is set on keeping your decrees to the very end.

PSALM 119:112

Are you determined to continue eating the way God wants you to eat until the very end—until you reach your proper weight? Set your heart today. Make a commitment to persevere until the goal is reached!

_____

_____

_____

_____

_____

_____

P-Attitudes

PERFECTION

Worried that you won't be perfect in your walk? Stop worrying about it—you *won't* be perfect! God knows that you won't be perfect; He knows you will have moments of weakness, but He says that His power is made perfect in your weakness, so forget perfection and plug in to His power!

2 CORINTHIANS 12:9

How sweet are your words to my taste,
sweeter than honey to my mouth!

PSALM 119:103

ot a sweet tooth? Before it gets out of control, try "eating" some of God's word. You just might find that His words are sweeter than honey—and they are nonfattening, too!

_____

_____

_____

_____

_____

_____

Though I knew Jesus as my Savior and was sure that He could help me with my eating problems, I was unable to overcome my obsession with food. I went through just about every method of control there is—dieting, fasting, exercise, and purging—only to see the compulsive eating return with a vengeance, along with feelings of failure.

Then in March of 1996, our church offered the Weigh Down Workshop™. I was ready to try yet another weight loss method. The first week hit me with such power because I found the missing key—admitting that overeating was displeasing to God. I repented and asked His forgiveness. At that moment I was released from slavery to food.

The Lord continued to bless and the weight came off, at one pound a week—the slowest I ever lost weight, but I believe it was for a purpose. Never had I been so satisfied on so little food! I could eat this way forever! Just 45 weeks later, I was at goal weight—and so free!

Every time I felt that I was not doing as well as I had been, I would ask the Lord, "Is there something in the way?" And He would reveal it to me—procrastination, laziness, self-degradation, and so on. Systematically He freed me from these things.

He has taken a useless vessel (me) and made it useful to Him. I find much fulfillment in sharing my faith and the Lord's great power with others who are in the same prison to food that I had been. He is faithful to deliver! Jesus is the answer to everything.

One of my favorite verses is:

> "For this very reason, make every effort to add to your faith goodness; and to goodness, knowledge; and to knowledge, self-control; and to self-control, perseverance; and to perseverance, godliness; and to godliness, brotherly kindness; and to brotherly kindness, love. For if you possess these qualities in increasing measure, they will keep you from being ineffective and unproductive in your knowledge of our Lord Jesus Christ."

2 PETER 1:5–8

Debby F.

A cheerful heart is good medicine,
but a crushed spirit dries up the bones.

PROVERBS 17:22

Dieting is no excuse for self-pity. Feeling sorry for yourself will only "dry up your bones." Instead, cultivate a cheerful heart. Be happy that you are pleasing God and that you are working toward your goal.

P-Attitudes

PASTURES

EVER THOUGHT ABOUT PASTURES IN THE DESERT? WHERE DO YOU THINK THE CAMELS GRAZE? TAKE TIME TO DO A LITTLE GRAZING YOURSELF IN THE DESERT PASTURES. CHEW ON THE TRUTH OF GOD'S WORD AND DRINK A BIT OF THE LIVING WATER, THEN CONTINUE ON YOUR JOURNEY, FED AND REFRESHED!

PSALM 23:2

If you put away the sin that is in your hand and allow no evil to dwell in your tent, then you will lift up your face without shame; you will stand firm and without fear.

JOB 11:14–15

Don't be caught "red-handed!" Get that food out of your hand and out of your mind, then you can hold your head high, without shame. You will stand firm—and have a firm body to boot!

_____

_____

_____

_____

_____

_____

_____   _____

P-Attitudes

PERFORMANCE

ARE YOU OPERATING AT PEAK PERFORMANCE? OR ARE YOU JUST HOBBLING THROUGH THE DESERT, HOPING TO ARRIVE AT YOUR DESTINATION? IT MAY BE TIME FOR A SPIRITUAL *TUNE-UP*! TAKE A DAY OR TWO AND PLACE YOURSELF IN THE CARE OF THE MASTER MECHANIC. SPEND TIME IN THE WORD AND IN PRAYER, ASKING GOD TO "REV UP YOUR ENGINE." THEN GET BACK OUT THERE AND *BURN RUBBER*!

COLOSSIANS 2:7

Let the wicked forsake his way and the evil man his thoughts.
Let Him turn to the LORD, and He will have mercy on him,
and to our God, for He will freely pardon.

ISAIAH 55:7

So you blew it—don't let that be enough to make you give up your dreams. Turn to the Lord, He will have mercy on you; He will freely pardon you. He doesn't want you to give up!

P-Attitudes

PERSECUTION

ONE OF THE TOUGHEST THINGS TO DO IS TO REMAIN FAITHFUL TO WHAT YOU KNOW IS RIGHT IN THE FACE OF PERSECUTION. DON'T FALL BACK ON YOUR OLD HABITS OF RUNNING TO FOOD WHEN THE PRESSURE IS ON. INSTEAD, THROW BACK YOUR SHOULDERS AND STICK OUT YOUR CHIN AND WALK WITH DETERMINATION IN WHAT YOU KNOW IS RIGHT!

ROMANS 8:35

Whether you turn to the right or to the left, your ears will hear a voice behind you, saying, "This is the way; walk in it."

ISAIAH 30:21

Diets come and go, but eating the way God planned for you to eat never changes. When you are in doubt about which eating plan is best, listen for God's voice to direct you.

_____

_____

_____

_____

_____

_____

_____

Don't we have the right to food and drink?

I CORINTHIANS 9:4

We have the right to eat and drink—whatever, whenever we want and it's this overexercised right which has piled on the pounds. In fact, this may be the only thing in our lives which is *overexercised*!

We can't blame diets, friends, a bad childhood, glands, or poverty as the cause for our being overweight. We may have been taught bad eating habits, we may have had a rough childhood, and we may have been dealt a hard hand in life, but we cannot continue to use this as an excuse to overeat.

Until we accept full responsibility for the eating choices we make, we will never overcome overeating. No one lifts the food to our mouths and forces us to swallow. We make that choice for ourselves. When we go through rough times, we choose to turn to the fridge instead of to the Lord. We choose to dive into a bag of chips instead of into the Word of God.

While this is a hard pill to swallow, the good news is that once we accept the responsibility for our choices—we can exercise our right to eat by making wise eating choices—choices which will lead to a thinner, healthier body.

What about it—are you ready to accept responsibility for yourself? Are you ready to start exercising your right to eat wisely? It's your choice. It's your right. How are you going to use it today?

So do not throw away your confidence;
it will be richly rewarded. You need to persevere
so that when you have done the will of God,
you will receive what He has promised.

Hebrews 10:35–36

If you have a lot of weight to lose, you may find yourself thinking you might never make it to your goal. Don't throw away your confidence! God promises that if you persevere, you will be richly rewarded!

P-Attitudes

PIZZAZZ

LET'S DO THIS THING WITH A LITTLE PIZZAZZ! DON'T WAIT UNTIL ALL YOUR WEIGHT HAS COME OFF TO DRESS WITH STYLE. START NOW TO CARRY YOURSELF WITH GRACE AND DIGNITY. YOU MAY AS WELL GET USED TO LOOKING GREAT!

PROVERBS 31:25

No discipline seems pleasant at the time, but painful.
Later on, however, it produces a harvest of righteousness
and peace for those who have been trained by it.

HEBREWS 12:11

*D*isciplining your appetite can be tiring work, sometimes even painful, but it will be well worth the trouble when you see the harvest it will produce—so stick with it!

_____

_____

_____

_____

_____

_____

P-Attitudes

POUTING

Is that you hiding in the crevice of a desert rock, pouting because you can't eat like you used to? Are you sullen because the weight isn't coming off fast enough to suit you? Snap out of it! Put a smile on that face because the Lord is shaping you into the image of His Son. He may be busy working on the inside first, but the outside will not be left undone!

PSALM 42:5

Is this the way you repay the LORD,
O foolish and unwise people? Is He not your Father,
your Creator, who made you and formed you?

DEUTERONOMY 32:6

God is our Father, our Creator. He made us and formed us. Should we repay Him by allowing foolish and unwise eating habits to destroy the body He created for us? Let's respond to Him by caring for our bodies.

_____

_____

_____

_____

_____

_____

P-Attitudes

PRIORITIES

WHICH COMES FIRST—YOUR DESIRE TO LOSE WEIGHT OR YOUR DESIRE TO GROW IN CHRIST? IF YOUR MAIN FOCUS IS ON TAKING OFF THE POUNDS, YOU HAVE MISSED THE POINT. IT'S ONLY AS YOU DRAW CLOSER TO THE LORD THAT HE GIVES YOU THE POWER AND DETERMINATION TO OVERCOME THE SIN OF OVEREATING. WE MUST GET OUR PRIORITIES IN LINE.

MATTHEW 6:25

Consider it pure joy, my brothers, whenever you face trials of many kinds, because you know that the testing of your faith develops perseverance.

JAMES 1:2–3

We seldom consider temptation a joy, but it can be. We know that each time we overcome the temptation, our faith is being strengthened. Just count the trial as one more opportunity to show your devotion to God by resisting.

---

*But Daniel resolved not to defile himself
with the royal food and wine, and he asked the chief official
for permission not to defile himself this way.*

DANIEL 1:8

Daniel knew the importance of sticking with the eating plan that he felt God had given to him. Though he was offered the finest food in the land—food fit for a king, he refused it. Oh, that we would do the same!

Are you as determined as Daniel? No matter what the "experts" say, no matter what your family says, no matter what "royal food" is set before you, if you know in your heart that God has called you to eat a certain way—stick to your guns!

God's way is always best, because He knows each of us individually. The kinds of food you may crave may not be the best foods to nourish your body. Each person deals with a variety of medical conditions which may call for different types of nourishment. God knows this and is perfectly capable of "custom designing" an eating plan for your individual needs.

Ask God what are the best types of foods for you to eat, how often you should eat, and what quantities to eat, then once you *know* that you have heard from Him, stick with it, no matter what!

Some of you may be wondering if this goes against the teachings we have been following—I don't think so. Gwen consistently teaches us to go to God, to seek His will and to be obedient to what He tells us, and that's exactly what we are doing!

I confess my iniquity; I am troubled by my sin.

PSALM 38:18

Does it bother you when you overeat? Good! Overeating is a sin, and we should always be bothered by sin. Let those guilty feelings pull you to your knees in prayer, and they will quickly go away.

P-Attitudes

PORTIONS

Are you being careful about your portions? I'm not just talking about your food portions—are you being sure to get your daily portion of reading God's Word and spending time with Him in prayer? All these things work together to help you reach your goal.

PSALM 119:57

My mouth is filled with your praise,
declaring your splendor all day long.

PSALM 71:8

What's your mouth filled with? Is it filled with praise for God or with chocolate chip cookies? Let's declare the splendor of the Lord all day long—let's fill our mouths with the right stuff!

_____

_____

_____

_____

_____

_____

_____

P-Attitudes

PROCRASTINATION

How long do you wait before you do what you know the Lord is telling you to do? Procrastination will cripple your progress. The only thing you are *putting off* is victory! Be swift to obey the Lord in all things.

LUKE 24:25

Then I acknowledged my sin to you and did not cover up my iniquity. I said, "I will confess my transgressions to the LORD"—and you forgave the guilt of my sin.

PSALM 32:5

Don't cover up when you blow it—confess it to the Lord and He will forgive you. Don't bother to hide the candy wrappers, empty chip bags, or pastry boxes. He already saw you! (Selah means stop and think about it.)

_____

_____

_____

_____

_____

_____

_____

P-Attitudes

PROSE

Did you ever write a poem to God? Pull up a desert rock and take time to do it now. It doesn't have to rhyme, it doesn't have to be great—it just has to speak from your heart. Take time for a little "Desert Prose" today.

1 JOHN 1:4

Your eye is the lamp of your body. When your eyes are good,
your whole body also is full of light. But when they are bad,
your body also is full of darkness.

Luke 11:34

Constantly gazing into the pantry or refrigerator? This sets you up for a fall. Keep your eyes from leading you into darkness. Better still, keep your eyes on God and your whole body will be full of light!

_____

_____

_____

_____

_____

_____

I accepted the Lord later in my life than most. I was almost 30. From that time on, I sought His will for my life in every area—family problems, finances, relationships, health—everything, but it never had occurred to me to seek His help to lose weight.

Then I came across the Weigh Down™ Diet book by Gwen Shamblin and thought, "No way. I am never going to diet again." I had read many diet books and they were full of do this, don't do this, eat this, don't eat that—too many restrictions for me, but this book seemed to hit me right between the eyes. The problem wasn't *what* I was eating; it was *why* I was eating. Food was comfort; it was a friend that was always there when I needed a friend; it was a pick-me-up when I felt low and it was a calm-me-down when I felt keyed up. I had made food an idol and wasn't even aware of it!

Through the program, I have had many blessings, the best of which is that after all these years, I have experienced a more loving, personal, intimate relationship with Him than I ever dreamed possible. I want to serve Him. I want to obey Him. Before Weigh Down™, I just wanted to be a "part" of His family, but not necessarily an active part. My attitude has changed completely. He has opened up new ways for me to serve Him; ways that before the program I would have been too scared or intimidated to try. Coordinating a Weigh Down™ group is one example, giving me the opportunity to encourage others.

I guess the most valuable benefit of the Weigh Down™ program for me is learning that I really can't do anything on my own. I don't have the talent, ability, desire or motivation; He has put those things in me. Oh yes, I did lose weight. I've lost over 40 pounds and have gone from a size 18 to an 8.

Proverbs 16:3 says "Commit to the Lord whatever you do, and your plans will succeed." I don't know what else He has in store for me, but I do know that He is faithful. I know that I can trust Him. I know that where He leads, I will follow.

Debbie H.

LORD, you have assigned me my portion and my cup; you have made my lot secure.

Psalm 16:5

Are you satisfied with your portion, or do you clean up the leftovers as you clear the table? Remember to be content with the portion God has allotted you and leave the rest to the garbage disposal!

P-Attitudes

PILLARS

When the children of Israel made their exodus from Egypt, the Lord led them through the desert with a pillar of fire, but did you know that you will some day be made a pillar in the house of God? Read the exciting promise for yourself.

REVELATION 3:12

So, if you think you are standing firm,
be careful that you don't fall!

1 CORINTHIANS 10:12

If you have been experiencing success in losing weight, but haven't quite reached your goal, be careful. It's easy to slack off, thinking that you are doing well, and get off track. Watch you don't fall!

_____

_____

_____

_____

_____

_____

_____   _____

P-Attitudes

PRESSURE

We all face the pressures of life, but we don't have to let them stress us out. I remember Mom cooking with a pressure cooker. The little valve on the top wiggled and jiggled as it released the pressure so the pot wouldn't explode. We must do the same; release your pressure to the Lord.

2 CORINTHIANS 4:8–10

"Let us eat and drink, for tomorrow we die."
Do not be misled: "Bad company corrupts good character."

1 Corinthians 15:32b, 33

Hanging out with the crowd who likes to "pig out" is bad news. Don't let others persuade you to eat more than you should. Remember that bad company corrupts good character!

_____

_____

_____

_____

_____

_____

_____

P-Attitudes

PARTICIPATION

God wants to help you take your weight off, but it will take your participation to get it done. Be careful you don't fall into the trap of thinking it's God's job to take the weight off. He will do it, but you must fully participate in the process by staying obedient with your eating.

2 PETER 1:4

For physical training is of some value, but godliness has value for all things, holding promise for both the present life and the life to come.

1 TIMOTHY 4:8

Physical exercise is a great way to keep your body healthy, but living a godly life benefits us both in this present life and in the life to come, so be sure to include a spiritual workout in your day.

*He who is full loathes honey, but to the hungry
even what is bitter tastes sweet.*

PROVERBS 27:7

Ain't it the truth! When I'm full, nothing sounds good and when I'm hungry, *everything* sounds good. I guess that's why they say you should never do your grocery shopping when you are hungry.

Unfortunately, just because food doesn't sound good when I'm full, that doesn't always stop me from eating! I will wander from the fridge to the pantry muttering, "I'm hungry, but I don't know what I want." (Come on, you've been there—done that!) Finally, I grab something that sounds good, but, after I've eaten it, I am seldom satisfied. It never tastes as good as I thought it would. (Am I right?)

On the other hand, when I am truly hungry, everything sounds and tastes good—even veggies! Hmmm . . . I guess that's the point of waiting until I'm truly hungry to eat. Gee, this whole thing really does make sense!

I intend to use this revelation to help me distinguish real hunger from head hunger. For instance, if I think I'm hungry, but nothing really sounds good, I will know I'm not really hungry. Then I can find something else to occupy my mind—reading the Bible,

exercise, cleaning, surfing the Web—anything but eating! Sounds like good strategy to me . . . how about you?

So, as the Holy Spirit says: "Today, if you hear his voice, do not harden your hearts as you did in the rebellion, during the time of testing in the desert, . . ."

HEBREWS 3:7–8

Many times you will hear God whisper, "You don't need that," just as you are about to eat a snack between meals. Don't harden your heart. Don't rebel against His instructions. Put it back!

P-Attitudes

PATHS

THERE ARE MANY PATHS IN THE DESERT, BUT
ONLY ONE THAT WILL LEAD YOU ON A DIRECT
ROUTE TO THE PROMISED LAND. WATCH THAT
YOU DON'T GET SIDETRACKED DOWN A PATH
THAT WILL LENGTHEN THE TIME OF YOUR
JOURNEY. FOLLOW ONLY THE SIGNS MARKED
"OBEDIENCE."

JOB 24:13

The sluggard's craving will be the death of him,
because his hands refuse to work.

PROVERBS 21:25

*E*ver notice how lying around the house leads to boredom, which leads to a craving to eat? Get off that sofa and get busy working with your hands to stave off that craving. You'll be glad you did!

_____

_____

_____

_____

_____

_____

P-Attitudes

PICNICS

Don't forget to stop along the way and enjoy the journey. Spread a table under a big old tree and enjoy a meal with the Lord from time to time. This journey can be fun if we make it that way.

1 KINGS 19:5

*It is the LORD your God you must follow,
and Him you must revere. Keep His commands and obey Him;
serve Him and hold fast to Him.*

DEUTERONOMY 13:4

Remember that childhood game, Follow the Leader? God is the leader, let's follow Him. If we must mimic anyone, let it be the Lord our God, not the "weight loss experts" of this generation! Who's your leader?

_____

_____

_____

_____

_____

_____

_____

P-Attitudes

PAIN

EACH OF US WILL EXPERIENCE SOME PAIN IN OUR LIVES AND EACH WILL COPE WITH IT A DIFFERENT WAY. IN THE PAST WE HAVE TRIED TO COVER THE PAIN BY COMFORTING OURSELVES WITH FOOD. IT DIDN'T WORK. WANT TO KNOW WHAT DOES WORK? RUN TO YOUR HEAVENLY FATHER AND ALLOW HIM TO SOOTHE THE PAIN AWAY!

REVELATION 21:4

Forgetting what is behind and straining toward what is ahead,
I press on toward the goal to win the prize
for which God has called me heavenward in Christ Jesus.

PHILIPPIANS 3:13B–14

*F*ailed at losing weight in the past? Forget it! Messed up yesterday?
Forget it! Blew it an hour ago? Forget it! Confess it, repent and
forget it. Then press on toward the goal.

*And a highway will be there; it will be called the
Way of Holiness. The unclean will not journey on it;
it will be for those who walk in that Way;
wicked fools will not go about on it.*

ISAIAH 35:8

One of my favorite poems has a line that goes "Two roads diverged in a wood, and I, I took the one less traveled by . . . and that has made all the difference."

I have always fancied myself a bit of an adventurer. If all the world was taking the path to the left—the well-worn and proven path, then I wanted to take the path to the right—the one with overgrown weeds, the uncertain path—the road less traveled.

If you are a Christian and you are striving to be all that God wants you to be, you will find yourself on a highway called the Way of Holiness. This path goes in the opposite direction as the well-worn path taken by most of the world. Millions are *dieting* right now to lose weight, but you have chosen a different way—God's way.

That's not to say that it's the easy way; in fact, just the opposite may be true. Sometimes we feel more comfortable clinging to a written set of diet rules, but God wants us to be daring enough to step off that well-worn road to nowhere and dare to follow Him. Will you do that?

Whatever you do, work at it with all your heart,
as working for the LORD, not for men, . . .

Colossians 3:23a

Eat right, do it with all your heart and do it for the Lord—not for your husband, your children, your mother, or even for yourself, but because you want to please the Lord.

P-Attitudes

PARADISE

Keep your eyes on the goal! All that you do in obedience to God leads you one step closer to the paradise He has prepared for you. Your future holds the promise of eternity in Paradise with your maker; nothing here on earth is greater than that.

REVELATION 2:7

Therefore, as God's chosen people, holy and dearly loved,
clothe yourselves with compassion, kindness, humility,
gentleness and patience. Bear with each other
and forgive whatever grievances you may have against
one another. Forgive as the LORD forgave you.

COLOSSIANS 3:12–13

Unforgiveness leads to anger, anger to bitterness, bitterness to depression and depression leads to the pantry! Better to forgive and get rid of the depression that eats at you, than to eat in order to rid yourself of the depression!

P-Attitudes

PATIENCE

IF YOU HAVE A LOT OF WEIGHT TO LOSE, IT MAY SEEM LIKE IT WILL TAKE FOREVER TO GET IT OFF. KEEP A STEADY COURSE, AN EVEN PACE, AND A STEADFAST DETERMINATION TO REACH YOUR GOAL AND IT WILL HAPPEN. PATIENCE IS THE KEY TO VICTORY!

HEBREWS 6:12

You are my lamp, O LORD;
the LORD turns my darkness into light.

2 Samuel 22:29

Got the blues? Don't feed them, they will grow! Instead, break that gloominess by turning on the lights—literally! Flood your house with light, throw back the curtains, turn on the lamps, grab your Bible and read—break through that blue funk!

_____

_____

_____

_____

_____

_____

_____

P-Attitudes

PANIC

GAINED A POUND? DON'T PANIC! WEIGHT FLUCTUATIONS ARE NORMAL. IT DOESN'T MEAN THAT YOU ARE NOT LOSING WEIGHT. AS LONG AS YOU ARE EATING ONLY WHEN HUNGRY AND STOPPING JUST SHORT OF FULL, YOU WILL LOSE THOSE EXCESS POUNDS AND RETURN TO YOUR NORMAL WEIGHT.

DEUTERONOMY 20:3B

For the kingdom of God is not a matter of eating and drinking,
but of righteousness, peace and joy in the Holy Spirit.

ROMANS 14:17

Sometimes eating and drinking can seem much more important than they really are. God would rather you concentrate on righteousness, peace and joy in the Holy Spirit than on what you will have for dinner.

In late 1996, I found myself more than 60 pounds over my wedding weight. I cried frequently and hated to look at myself in the mirror. I couldn't bend over to tie my shoes—I couldn't even see them when I stood up! In short, I was a very unhappy camper.

One day, my boss was trying to explain something while I was eating popcorn. As I shoveled it in, she became frustrated and said, "Elaine, don't worry about the popcorn right now!" I was horrified and realized that I was obsessed with food and I needed help!

I heard about the Weigh Down Workshop™ from one of the ladies at our church. It was a wonderful program she said that focused on God. I argued with myself about the cost of the session. After all, I am a single mom with very limited funds. Another friend told me that she would be attending the upcoming session and asked if I would go with her. I told her I'd think about it. When she called again, I made excuses. I told her I would "love" to do it but that Wednesday nights were bad for me and that I just couldn't afford the fee.

The very next day, I got the mail and saw an envelope with no return address. Inside was a money order for $100 and nothing else. No note of explanation—nothing. I started to think about how I could spend the money. As I closed the front door, the thought came to me—Weigh Down Workshop™. I WAS ANGRY! I think that I even stomped my feet, looked up toward heaven and said (through clenched teeth), "Alright! I'll do it."

While I didn't embrace the idea with joy and smiles, the Lord honored my commitment. I lost 35 or 40 pounds during the first session and over 20 pounds in the second. In all, the Lord has removed 60+ pounds from my frame and He has reduced my size from 14–16 to 4–6. But that is not the best thing—my heart was renewed, and I am more in love with the Lord than I have been in a long time. My depression lifted, and I marvel at the face I now see in the mirror. To God be the Glory!

Elaine L.

Now what I am commanding you today
is not too difficult for you or beyond your reach.

DEUTERONOMY 30:11

God never commands us to do something that is too difficult for us to accomplish. You can lose those pounds, you can wait for hunger before you eat, and you can stop when you've had just enough. Trust God.

P-Attitudes

PEARLS

Keep your eyes open for pearls in the desert—jewels of blessing dropped in your lap by God as a reward for your obedience. He delights in giving His children the desires of their heart, so watch for the blessings!

PSALM 128:2

Since, then, you have been raised with Christ,
set your hearts on things above, where Christ is seated
at the right hand of God. Set your minds on things above,
not on earthly things.

COLOSSIANS 3:1–2

What's your heart and mind set on? Is it food or God? Fill your mind with the Word, fill your time by doing things for others, fill your heart with love and let God worry about filling your tummy!

_____

_____

_____

_____

_____

_____

P-Attitudes

PECULIARITY

Okay, fair warning—people are going to think you are peculiar. They won't understand the concept of eating regular foods (not low-fat, low-calorie) while you are losing weight. Don't worry about being peculiar. Your emerging thin body will be your reward!

1 PETER 4:3-4

*The LORD your God is testing you to find out whether you
love Him with all your heart and with all your soul.*

DEUTERONOMY 13:3B

God calls us to obedience to test us, to find out whether we love
Him with all our heart and soul. Are you passing the test?

_____

_____

_____

_____

_____

_____

P-Attitudes

PERISHING

You aren't perishing! Waiting for true hunger may make you think you are going to *perish*, but believe me, you won't die. Soon you will be able to forget about food entirely until your tummy growls to let you know it's time for a meal. So don't worry, you aren't perishing.

JOHN 10:28

Here I am! I stand at the door and knock.
If anyone hears my voice and opens the door,
I will come in and eat with him, and he with me.

REVELATION 3:20

What better dinner guest to have than the Lord Himself? Why not open the door and invite Him to dine with you at your next meal? I bet you won't overeat!

_____

_____

_____

_____

_____

_____

*"Everything is permissible for me"—but not everything
is beneficial. "Everything is permissible for me"—but I will not
be mastered by anything. "Food for the stomach and the
stomach for food"—but God will destroy them both.*

1 Corinthians 6:12–13a

We are reminded once again that though we are free to eat any-thing, we must be careful that this freedom doesn't become an excuse to freely indulge in our every whim. We are to tame our flesh—not cater to it. Remember, it says here that we are not to let ourselves be *mastered* by anything.

If there are certain foods which *master* us, then we must avoid them until we have gained enough self-discipline to take control. This may seem out of place with the "eat whatever you want" philosophy, but it's really not. It's just using the good sense that God gave us to avoid temptation. We wouldn't set a beer in front of an alcoholic, nor a cigarette before someone trying to quit, so let's not make it harder on ourselves. If there is a particular food that "sets us off," let's avoid it for now. We can have it later when we have more self-control.

Every day we are getting stronger. Soon food will have no control over us, but until then, let's use a little common sense when making food choices.

Dear friends, do not be surprised at the painful trial you are suffering, as though something strange were happening to you. But rejoice that you participate in the sufferings of Christ, . . .

1 PETER 4:12–13A

Some believe that losing weight with God will be a piece of cake. (Pun intended!) Surprise, surprise—this walk can sometimes be painful. But don't let that get you down—rejoice that you are following in the footsteps of Christ.

P-Attitudes

PREDICAMENTS

PARTIES, SMORGASBORDS, WEDDINGS, DINNER DATES, BUSINESS LUNCHEONS, SUNDAYS WITH MOM . . . ALL PREDICAMENTS THAT CAN LEAD TO DISOBEDIENT EATING. BEWARE OF THEM AND BE PREPARED FOR THEM.

1 CORINTHIANS 10:12

Peace I leave with you; my peace I give you.
I do not give to you as the world gives.
Do not let your hearts be troubled and do not be afraid.

JOHN 14:27

I've heard people say they are afraid to lose weight for one reason or another. Don't let your hearts be troubled or fearful, God will work it all out and fill you with His perfect peace in the process!

_____

_____

_____

_____

_____

_____

_____

P-Attitudes

PRIDE

PRIDE IS A TWO-EDGED SWORD. IF WE BECOME PRIDEFUL OF OUR WEIGHT LOSS, OUR SLIM-MER BODY OR INCREDIBLE SELF-CONTROL, WE ARE SETTING OURSELVES UP FOR A FALL. ON THE OTHER HAND, BEING PROUD OF WHO WE ARE IN CHRIST AND WHAT HE IS ACCOMPLISH-ING IN US IS PERFECTLY ACCEPTABLE.

PROVERBS 16:18

So we fix our eyes not on what is seen, but on what is unseen.
For what is seen is temporary, but what is unseen is eternal.

2 CORINTHIANS 4:18

Don't be discouraged by the scales or the mirror at first—remember, what you see now is only temporary, but what God is doing in you, both physically and spiritually is eternal!

_____

_____

_____

_____

_____

_____   _____

P-Attitudes

PEBBLES

I ONCE HEARD OF A COORDINATOR WHO GREETED EACH MEMBER OF THE GROUP BY GIVING THEM A PEBBLE TO PUT IN THEIR SHOE. SHE INSTRUCTED THEM TO WALK AROUND THE ROOM A BIT AND THEN OFFERED EACH PERSON A CANDY BAR SAYING, "HERE, THIS WILL MAKE THE PAIN GO AWAY." RIDICULOUS TO THINK CANDY CAN TAKE AWAY PAIN, RIGHT? I THINK YOU GET THE PICTURE— FOOD CAN NOT COMFORT US, THAT'S GOD'S JOB.

2 CORINTHIANS 1:3–4

Praise be to the God and Father of our LORD Jesus Christ,
the Father of compassion and the God of all comfort, . . .

2 CORINTHIANS 1:3

Repeat after me . . . food can never comfort me the way God can. Stop running to food when you need comfort. Only the Father of compassion and the God of all comfort is able to bring us true peace.

But the fruit of the Spirit is love, joy, peace, patience, kindness, goodness, faithfulness, gentleness and self-control.

GALATIANS 5:22–23A

I keep hearing that we should be eating more fruit. It's full of vitamins and fiber and will satisfy our sweet tooth without doing damage to our system the way refined sugar does.

Isn't the fruit of the Spirit just like that? Love, joy, peace, patience, kindness, goodness, faithfulness, gentleness—such sweet sounding words. Just saying them, reading them, is like picking up a fully ripe peach and catching a whiff of its delectable, mouth-watering fragrance. Yes, I think I should like eating more of this kind of fruit.

Oops! I seem to have left one of the fruits out . . . the last one in the list is self-control! Is it just me or does this one seem out of place among all the rest? Sort of like the pit right in the middle of that juicy, sweet peach. It's so hard and takes up so much space in the peach. Wouldn't it be better if there were no pit . . . only the yummy flesh of the peach?

But that pit is the very life of the peach. Without the pit, there would be no sweet fruit, because that pit is the source of the fruit. The life is in the pit!

So it is with self-control. This is the source, from which all the other fruits grow and blossom. Unless we accept self-control and

embrace it, we will not be able to experience the other fruits of the Spirit: love, joy, peace, patience, kindness, goodness, faithfulness, and gentleness. These can all be hindered if we insist on living without self-control.

I think the experts are right—we should be eating more fruit! I intend to incorporate all the fruits of the Spirit into my daily diet . . . starting with a generous helping of self-control!

Do everything without complaining or arguing,
so that you may become blameless and pure,
children of God without fault in a crooked and depraved
generation, in which you shine like stars in the universe . . .

PHILIPPIANS 2:14–15

Do everything without complaining or arguing—that includes eating right! It's hard to be a shining star for God when you argue and complain—so stop your grumbling!

P-Attitudes

PARTY

Look at your desert journey as a party—a celebration of your emancipation from the bondage of overeating. Rejoice over your freedom that you have to eat the foods you love, instead of eating diet foods. Dance, laugh and have a good time in the desert . . . it's a party!

ISAIAH 30:29

Do not conform any longer to the pattern of this world, but be transformed by the renewing of your mind.

ROMANS 12:2A

$\mathcal{D}$are to be different! Gather up all those diet books and appetite suppressants and throw them in the trash. Boldly step out of the path that everyone else is taking and dare to trust God to help you lose weight.

_____

_____

_____

_____

_____

_____

P-Attitudes

PEDESTALS

Beware of setting up pedestals in the desert, because as soon as you erect a pedestal, you must place something on it: the scales, certain foods, your leaders, yourself. It's better to build altars in the desert than to build pedestals. Things tend to fall off pedestals, but everything that is laid on the altar stays put.

GENESIS 35:3

Be self-controlled and alert. Your enemy the devil
prowls around like a roaring lion
looking for someone to devour.

1 PETER 5:8

The devil can't make you give into temptation; he can only place it before you and hope you will cooperate. Don't give him the satisfaction!

_____

_____

_____

_____

_____

_____

P-Attitudes

PIONEER

Eating God's way is totally different from every diet you have been on. You are a pioneer in this revolutionary way to return to and maintain your normal weight, so when others tell you, "That's not the way it's done," you can say, "It is now, I'm a pioneer in the process!"

ISAIAH 43:19

Therefore, prepare your minds for action; be self-controlled; set your hope fully on the grace to be given you when Jesus Christ is revealed.

1 Peter 1:13

Facing a party or banquet? Prepare your mind for action! Decide beforehand that you will eat in obedience to God and trust Him to give you the grace you need to stick to it.

_____

_____

_____

_____

_____

_____

At 305 pounds, I had sleep apnea, high blood pressure, aching joints, acid reflux and severe depression. I had given up trying to lose weight. I knew I couldn't diet for the rest of my life, and I saw no point in losing weight only to gain it all back.

One day a friend said she had a weight loss tape she thought I should hear. I knew it wouldn't help, but I took it so I wouldn't offend her. The next morning I popped the tape in and started puttering around the house. I really wasn't paying much attention to it as I headed toward the bathroom to do some laundry when suddenly the voice on the tape said, "Now you put that laundry down and listen to me!" I dropped the armful of laundry and went to the tape player laughing because I knew that I had just been the victim of God-incidence (although I wasn't familiar with that term at that time). By the time the tape finished I was hooked.

The Weigh Down™ program made sense, and it seemed like something that I might be able to live with forever. There were no classes in my area, so my friend let me borrow one tape a week and wrote out the scripture references for me to look up. I wrote the scriptures out on scraps of paper and posted them all over my kitchen. If I felt like eating when I wasn't hungry, I took a *scripture tour*, reading all the posted notes and absorbing them as much as possible. It worked every time!

I grew much closer to the Lord and began to see that a whole new life was coming my way. I am now 170 pounds lighter and I'm amazed at the changes in me! I can shop in regular stores instead of Omar the tent maker's shop! I can sleep without any machinery to keep me breathing. I don't have to take blood pressure medication any more! I'm not so afraid of life and not so prone to depression.

I *know* that all I have to do is to keep on loving the Lord and following Him and all the other details of life will work out in His way and in His time.

Deb P.

Do you not know that in a race all the runners run,
but only one gets the prize? Run in such a way
as to get the prize.

1 Corinthians 9:24

Not everyone who sets out to lose weight reaches their goal. Don't let that happen to you. Run in such a way so as to get the prize—stay focused on the finish line!

P-Attitudes

PLATEAUS

Don't be surprised or disappointed when you find yourself on a desert plateau. Use the time to look around you at how far you've come. Rest a bit, then get right back on the road . . . look closely and you'll see the "No Parking" signs posted on the plateaus.

PSALM 143:10

Do not be anxious about anything, but in everything,
by prayer and petition, with thanksgiving,
present your requests to God.

PHILIPPIANS 4:6

Anxiety is unavoidable in these turbulent times. God knew that, so He provided a way for us to handle anxiety, and it's not found in food. Anxiety is to be handled with prayer and thanksgiving—not a knife and fork!

P-Attitudes

POSSIBILITIES

So many things that have been impossible for you are going to be possible now that you are eating right. The weight is coming off and you will be able to walk up stairs without being winded, eat a meal without antacids, and enjoy dessert without feeling guilty. Wake up to a world of possibilities as you eat obediently for the Lord.

MATTHEW 19:26

Jesus said to him, "Away from me, Satan! For it is written:
"Worship the LORD your God, and serve Him only."
Then the devil left Him, and angels came and attended Him.

MATTHEW 4:10–11

*E*ven Jesus was tempted by Satan. Jesus is our example. When temptation strikes, declare your devotion to God and watch the devil leave you as the angels come to attend you!

_____

_____

_____

_____

_____

_____

P-Attitudes

PERTURBED

Okay, so you're perturbed in the desert! A bit miffed that others seem to be eating so much more than you are able to eat. Ticked that you got all the "fat genes" while others can fit into designer jeans? God says *be slow to become angry,* because anger does not bring about the righteous life that God desires.

JAMES 1:19–20

So whether you eat or drink or whatever you do,
do it all for the glory of God.

1 Corinthians 10:31

God couldn't have said it any plainer than that! Everything we do, including what we eat and drink, should be done so that it will bring glory to God. Eat to please Him!

_____

_____

_____

_____

_____

_____

Therefore, my dear brothers, stand firm.
Let nothing move you. Always give yourselves fully
to the work of the LORD, because you know
that your labor in the LORD is not in vain.

1 CORINTHIANS 15:58

Stand firm—that's what we need to do! We must fix it in our minds that we are going to eat right no matter what the circumstances. We won't be moved by cravings, fast food drive-thrus, parties, picnics, emotions, boredom, or visits with Mom. In the face of all these things, we must stand firm in our determination to take off this excess weight!

We must give ourselves fully to eating the way God wants us to eat, knowing that our labor will not be in vain. We have spent too many years in self-indulgent eating—loving food so much that it was destroying our bodies, our relationships, and our effectiveness for God.

I don't know about you, but I am out to *prove* that I love God more than I love food. Not to prove it to anyone else, but to prove it to myself! I will conquer my untamed appetite! I will make it come under submission to God! I will stand firm and let nothing move me!

I will—will you?

"When he came to his senses, he said, 'How many of my father's hired men have food to spare, and here I am starving to death! . . .'"

LUKE 15:17

Have you spent years starving to death with diet after another? Come to your senses and realize that your Father, God has a perfect plan for attaining your proper weight. You'll be satisfied— with food to spare!

P-Attitudes

PLUCK

HAVE YOU GOT *PLUCK*? YOU KNOW—THAT CHEEKY DETERMINATION TO REACH YOUR GOALS IN SPITE OF WHATEVER OBSTACLES MAY LIE IN YOUR PATH? IF SO, THEN YOU ARE WELL ON YOUR WAY TO THE PROMISED LAND.

REVELATION 3:21

"But they all alike began to make excuses. . . ."

LUKE 14:18A

$\mathcal{D}$o you make excuses for your overeating? You were depressed, there was a party, or you just had to clean your plate. Honesty is the best policy—with yourself and with God. Don't make excuses. Nothing justifies rebellion.

P-Attitudes

PARTICULAR

Have you become particular about what you eat? Good! When you are eating according to God's plan (only when hungry) then you have every right to be particular about the foods you choose. Pick only those which you truly enjoy.

PROVERBS 21:20

"Why don't you judge for yourselves what is right? . . ."

LUKE 12:57

$\mathcal{A}$re you still listening to those "diet gurus" telling you how to lose weight? Why not seek wisdom from the "Ultimate Expert" (God), then judge for yourselves what is right? Which will it be— God's way or the world's way?

_____

_____

_____

_____

_____

_____

P-Attitudes

PIDDLING

My mother used to say, "Quit piddling around." This was usually said when I was taking way too long to do something she had told me to do. Are you piddling around in the desert? Taking way too long to do what God told you to do? You're only making your journey longer, so stop piddling!

PSALM 55:7–8

After he said this, he took some bread and gave thanks to God in front of them all. Then he broke it and began to eat.

ACTS 27:35

Do you say a prayer before you eat? Try this—thank God for the food and ask Him to let you know when to stop eating. Then enjoy your meal, but listen for God's voice to tell you when the meal is over.

_____

_____

_____

_____

_____

_____

_____

"... He must become greater, I must become less."

JOHN 3:30

John the Baptist made this statement. Just like John, who knew he must allow his ministry to diminish once Jesus had come on the scene, we must allow ourselves to diminish if Christ is to have free reign in our lives.

The first thing that comes to mind when we read this (since we are trying to lose weight) might be, "I would love to *diminish!*" Of course, we are thinking physically—God is thinking spiritually.

He knows that if we are to grow in Him, we must get ourselves out of the way. We must set our own will aside to make way for His will. This is tough to do, because like it or not, most of us are self-absorbed. We are consumed with our wants, needs, desires, plans, and goals. So, how can we become *less* so that He can become *more?*

Be a sponge! The more of Jesus we absorb, the less room there is for self-absorption. The hungrier we become for His standard of living, the less hungry we will be for food. The more our desire for Him increases, the less our own desires will coerce us into doing things we don't want to do.

So let's allow God to increase in our lives and then we will decrease—in more ways than one!

But now I urge you to keep up your courage,
because not one of you will be lost; . . .

Acts 27:22

Keep up your courage! You are not going to fail this time. You will reach your proper weight if you just keep going. Every one of us can count on God to get us there—not one will be lost if we just keep going!

P-Attitudes

PSALMS

Evenings are perfect for Psalms in the desert. Spread a soft blanket on the desert sand. Lay back and gaze into the starry sky and let your sweet songs of praise be carried on desert breezes to the Maker of heaven and earth.

COLOSSIANS 3:16

When they had eaten as much as they wanted,
they lightened the ship by throwing the grain into the sea.

ACTS 27:38

When you have had enough to eat, clear the table or walk away from it until everyone else is finished, then get the food out of sight. Throw it away or put it away so it won't tempt you.

_____

_____

_____

_____

_____

_____

_____

P-Attitudes

PURIFICATION

Did you know that water is purified as it sifts down through the sand, soil and rocks of the earth? Let this journey through the desert sift out any impurities you may have so that you might be a pleasing "drink of water" to the Lord.

1 PETER 1:22

Jesus said to them, "Come and have breakfast."

JOHN 21:12A

Lots of people skip breakfast, then overeat at lunchtime. After a full night's rest, the stomach is empty, so it's okay to eat breakfast—you might have missed the hunger signals while you were sleeping.

P-Attitudes

PROCLAMATIONS

WHAT DO YOU PROCLAIM IN THE DESERT? "I'LL NEVER BE ABLE TO LOSE THIS WEIGHT!" OR "I CAN DO ALL THINGS THROUGH CHRIST WHO GIVES ME STRENGTH!" THE WORDS OF OUR MOUTH DETERMINE THE ACTIONS WE TAKE, SO BE CAREFUL WHAT YOU PROCLAIM.

PSALM 19:14

"... But the world must learn that I love the Father
and that I do exactly what my Father has commanded me.
Come now; let us leave."

JOHN 14:31

Sometimes others will urge you to eat more than you should. When this happens, don't give in. It's time the world learns that you love the Father and that you intend to do exactly what He has commanded you to do.

I used to do okay with my eating on weekdays but totally blow it on the weekends. Just when I thought I had "gotten" it, a Saturday would roll around, my whole routine would change, and before I knew it I was eating out of control. Here's how I broke this cycle.

First, I make sure I do my daily devotional each morning before I eat anything (well, maybe with my coffee!). I take extra time to pray for God's strength to see me through the weekend. If a special event is going on, I ask Him to help me find true hunger and fullness during it. This has really helped me to stay focused on God and not on food.

Second, I plan my hunger. If I have a special event where I know there will be food, I plan to be hungry so I can eat when I get there. I just eat less at the previous meal so I can be hungry (not ravenous) for the party. I fill my plate, then eat, sip, talk, eat, sip, talk, and when I just START to feel satisfied I throw out my plate and get something to drink. This keeps my hands busy while others are still eating.

I have also found that when I take the time to serve others I spend less time thinking about food, so I busy myself with helping my kids with their plates. When I am at someone else's house, I like to help them with the dishes and my half-eaten plate is forgotten.

Many times I have overcome the temptation to eat when I am

not hungry by simply stating that *I am not hungry*. Most people don't have a problem with that. It's when you say you are *on a diet* that they just can't seem to leave you alone!

Well, I just wanted to share what works for me. I hope that it helps you. Remember to start your day with prayer and God will give you the strength that you ask for. My heart has been changed permanently and I owe it all to my Heavenly Father. He loves me!

Monica M.
P.S. He loves you too!

Surely God is my help;
the LORD is the one who sustains me.

PSALM 54:4

When you are in trouble, do you turn to food? Food cannot sustain you. It can do nothing to see you through your troubled times. It's the Lord who sustains you, so fill up on Him!

P-Attitudes

PROSPERITY

Did you know that prosperity comes when we are honest with God about our sin? His word says that when we cover up our sin, we will not prosper. Are you being perfectly honest with God about how you eat, or are you covering up?

PROVERBS 28:13

When the woman saw that the fruit of the tree was good for food and pleasing to the eye, and also desirable for gaining wisdom, she took some and ate it.

GENESIS 3:6

Just because food looks good, doesn't mean you should go against God's wishes and eat it. Just think what happened to Eve!

_____

_____

_____

_____

_____

_____

_____

P-Attitudes

PUDDLES

REMEMBER PLAYING IN PUDDLES WHEN YOU WERE SMALL? I THINK WE HAVE FORGOTTEN TO LOOK FOR THE SIMPLE PLEASURES OF LIFE. AS YOU MAKE YOUR WAY ACROSS THE DESERT, WATCH FOR OPPORTUNITIES TO *PLAY IN THE PUDDLES*!

PSALM 107:35

Everything that lives and moves will be food for you.
Just as I gave you the green plants,
I now give you everything.

GENESIS 9:3

What you eat is not nearly as important as how often you eat and how much you eat. God created all food, so eat what you like, but eat responsibly.

_____

_____

_____

_____

_____

_____

P-Attitudes

PRECISION

GOD IS NOT EARLY, NOR IS HE LATE, BUT HE IS PRECISELY ON TIME. LET'S IMITATE HIS PRECISION. LET'S NOT EAT TOO EARLY OR EAT TOO LATE, BUT EAT PRECISELY WHEN WE FEEL TRUE HUNGER. LET'S NOT EAT TOO MUCH OR EAT TOO LITTLE, BUT PRECISELY THE RIGHT AMOUNT.

PSALM 145:15

They all ate the same spiritual food and drank the same spiritual drink; for they drank from the spiritual rock that accompanied them, and that rock was Christ.

1 CORINTHIANS 10:3–4

There is something far more satisfying than physical food—it's spiritual food! The source of this spiritual food is Christ. Seek that food—in prayer and in Bible study, and physical food will not seem that important!

_____

_____

_____

_____

_____

_____

_____

*As Paul discoursed on righteousness, self-control
and the judgment to come, Felix was afraid and said,
"That's enough for now! You may leave.
When I find it convenient, I will send for you."*

ACTS 24:25

Felix reacted to Paul's preaching on righteousness and self-control just about the way we react when God broaches the subjects with us. He became afraid and said, "That's enough for now! You may leave. When I find it convenient, I will send for you."

What was he afraid of? That he might have to give up some worthless earthly pleasure? That he might have to change his lifestyle? His habits? That God might actually require him to move up to a higher standard of living? That if he did this he might lose a few friends?

Imagine—dismissing God the way Felix dismissed Paul! But that's exactly what we do when the Lord starts whispering to us about righteous living and self-control—we boot Him out! We tell Him that it's not convenient right now for us to make changes in our lives. Basically we dismiss God until we feel like sending for him again. And when is that? When we are in trouble of course!

How many times have we dismissed God when He talks to us about self-control in our eating? "Not convenient right now,

Lord . . . can't you see I'm stressed and need the food to calm my nerves?" "Self-control now? But this is a wedding celebration . . . look at all this food!" "Oh Father, I can't think about self-control now. After all, Mom made this special dinner just for me. She would be offended if I didn't eat plenty."

Then what do we do after we have ignored His warnings? We send for God! "Oh Father, I'm so miserable! Look how fat I have become. Why did you give me such a slow metabolism? Why did I inherit all my mother's fat genes? Why won't you help me lose weight?"

Felix, old buddy, thanks for holding the mirror up to our faces!

But food does not bring us near to God; we are no worse if we do not eat, and no better if we do.

1 Corinthians 8:8

Eating certain kinds of food (low-calorie, low-fat) does not make us more righteous or bring us closer to God. Only time spent in His presence will draw us into a closer relationship with Him.

P-Attitudes

PARABLES

Have you ever noticed how many times Jesus used parables to teach life's lessons? He still uses everyday occurrences to teach His people the deep truths of God. Keep your eyes open—He may be trying to teach you something today through the circumstances around you.

MATTHEW 13:10–11

The LORD answered, "Who then is the faithful and wise manager, whom the master puts in charge of his servants to give them their food allowance at the proper time? . . ."

LUKE 12:42

God expects us to be wise managers—to eat the proper amount of food at the proper time. If we are parents, we are to manage our children's food in the same way. Are you a wise manager?

_____

_____

_____

_____

_____

_____

_____

P-Attitudes

PLANTED

MANY PLANTS THRIVE IN THE DESERT, BUT ONLY IF THEIR ROOTS GROW DEEP ENOUGH TO REACH THE BURIED STREAMS OF WATER. ARE YOU PLANTED FIRMLY IN GOD? DO YOUR ROOTS GROW DEEP INTO THE DESERT SAND TO SEEK OUT THE STREAMS OF LIVING WATER, SO THAT YOU MIGHT GROW STRONG?

PSALM 1:1–3

"Life is more than food and the body more than clothes."

Luke 12:23

Life is about much more than what you will eat. If you are spending too much time thinking about eating, make a change. List the things that are most important in your life and fill your thoughts with them.

_____

_____

_____

_____

_____

_____

_____

P-Attitudes

PROTESTS

DON'T TELL ME YOU ARE ORGANIZING A PROTEST RALLY IN THE DESERT! DO I SEE YOU CARRYING A SIGN THAT READS *UNFAIR GENE DISTRIBUTION*? REMEMBER YOU ARE THE WORKMANSHIP OF GOD. HE CREATED YOU IN HIS OWN IMAGE, SO BURN THE SIGN, FORGET THE PROTESTS AND BE THE BEST YOU CAN BE FOR HIM!

PSALM 139:13–16

Blessed is the man who perseveres under trial,
because when he has stood the test, he will receive the crown of
life that God has promised to those who love Him.

JAMES 1:12

*H*ang tough, keep going, don't give up, continue, carry on, persist, and persevere—because when you do, you will receive the crown of life that God has promised to those who love Him. And you will reach your goal!

_____

_____

_____

_____

_____

_____

_____

Watch out that you do not lose what you have worked for, but that you may be rewarded fully.

2 JOHN 8

We have worked so hard to lose weight up to this point. It may be 2 pounds, it may be 102 pounds or anything in between, but we must be careful that we do not lose what we have worked for. Or in our case, that we do not gain what we have worked so hard to lose!

Why? Because God wants to fully reward us. He wants to see us make it all the way to the Promised Land—free from being controlled by food and free from relying on food to meet the needs that can only be met by Him. That's our reward for all the hard work of submitting our will to Him where eating is concerned. He doesn't want us to lose this reward.

How can we lose the reward? By easing up, by just this once, by just one more bite, by skipping our quiet time with Him, by neglecting prayer. The next thing you know, you stand on the scale in tears that all your hard work has been lost (or gained).

My friend, it's hard work to practice self-control, to surrender our will, to say no to ourselves. Let's not lose the reward we have worked so hard to gain by putting pounds back on. If you find yourself in that position, all is not lost (no pun intended). Just start over—begin working once again on obedience and stick with it so that you may be fully rewarded!

You save the humble, but your eyes are on the haughty to bring them low.

2 SAMUEL 22:28

Feeling proud of yourself because you lost a few pounds? Be careful to give God the glory for what He is doing in you. Don't allow yourself to be filled with pride, but walk humbly before the Lord.

P-Attitudes

PEACE

REMEMBER THAT GOD BRINGS PEACE IN THE MIDST OF THE STORM. WHEN THE HOT, DRY AIR BEGINS TO BLOW IN THE DESERT, WHIP- PING THE SAND INTO A SWIRLING SEA OF STING- ING NEEDLES, CALL ON THE ONE WHO CALMS THE STORM AND HE WILL BRING PEACE, SWEET PEACE.

MARK 4:39

If a man is lazy, the rafters sag;
if his hands are idle, the house leaks.

ECCLESIASTES 10:18

Are you being lazy about spending time in God's Word? Before long your spirit will sag and the strength will leak out of your walk. Break out of your laziness and get busy studying the Word of God!

_____

_____

_____

_____

_____

_____

P-Attitudes

PERSEVERANCE

Don't quit! Keep putting one sandal in front of the other . . . one step at a time is all it takes to complete the journey unless you quit walking. Each meal is a step. Make the right choice at each meal and before you know it you will have completed the journey!

HEBREWS 10:36

This is what the LORD says: "Restrain your voice from weeping and your eyes from tears, for your work will be rewarded," declares the LORD. "They will return from the land of the enemy. . . ."

JEREMIAH 31:16

Have you been working hard to eat right, but the scales aren't budging? Has it brought you to tears? Then dry those tears. God says He <u>will</u> reward your hard work, so you'll see results soon.

P-Attitudes

PARCHED

Feeling a bit dry, thirsty, parched? God's Word is like rain, like the dew of morning, like showers on new grass, like abundant rain—drink and be satisfied!

DEUTERONOMY 32:2

My flesh and my heart may fail, but God is the strength of my heart and my portion forever.

PSALM 73:26

Don't fuss over getting your daily portion of food. Rather, concentrate on getting your daily portion of God so that your heart may be full of strength for each day!

_____

_____

_____

_____

_____

_____

Well, we've come to the end of the book, but for many of us the journey is not over. We still have a few pounds to go before we reach our goal. Not to worry—I have just discovered that these Desert Morsels taste just as good the second and third time as they did with the first bite!

So turn back to page one and start again. Look closely, there might be some scrumptious tidbits you overlooked the first time. You might find that the Morsels you jotted down taste even better than mine did. Either way, there's plenty of spiritual food left to fuel the last leg of your journey. Dig into God's Word and discover the choice delicacies hidden there. Savor the flavor of a word from your Heavenly Father anytime you find yourself in need of a little nourishment.

I pray you have found some powerful truths in the P-attitudes and that they will play a part in helping you reach the Promised Land. God's promises are plenty and given to each of us personally, so plan to make the P-attitudes a part of your daily portion as you walk with our precious Savior.

I'll be praying for you!

Love in Christ,

Jan

Desert Morsels
Jan Christiansen

> Subtitled: *A Journal with Encouraging Tidbits from My Journey on the Weigh Down™ Diet*
>
> When Jan Christiansen set out to lose weight on the Weigh Down™ Diet she got more than she bargained for! In addition to losing over 35 pounds and gaining a closer relationship with God, Jan discovered a gift—her ability to entertain and comfort fellow dieters! Jan's inspiring website led to the release of her best-selling first book, *More of Him, Less of Me*. Now, Jan serves another helping of her wit and His wisdom in this lovely companion journal. Includes inspiring scripture, insightful comments, stories from readers, room for the reader's personal reflection and *Plenty of **Attitude*** (p-attitude).
>
> (cloth) ISBN 1892016214 **$17.95**

More of Him, Less of Me
Jan Christiansen

> Subtitled: *A Daybook of My Personal Insights, Inspirations & Meditations on the Weigh Down™ Diet*
>
> The insight shared in this yearlong daybook of inspiration will encourage you on your weight loss journey, bring you to a deeper relationship with God, and help you improve any facet of your life. Each page includes an essay, scripture, and a tip-of-the-day that will encourage and uplift you as you trust God to help you achieve your proper weight. Perfect companion guide for anyone on the Weigh Down™ diet!
>
> (cloth) ISBN 1892016001 **$17.95**

God Stories
Donna I. Douglas

> Subtitled: *They're So Amazing, Only God Could Make Them Happen*
>
> Famous individuals share their personal, true-life experiences with God in this beautiful new book! Find out how God has touched the lives of top recording artists, professional athletes, and other newsmakers like Jessi Colter, Deana Carter, Ben Vereen, Stephanie Zimbalist, Cindy Morgan, Sheila E., Joe Jacoby, Cheryl Landon, Brett Butler, Clifton Taulbert, Babbie Mason, Michael Medved, Sandi Patty, Charlie Daniels, and more! Their stories are intimate, poignant, and sure to inspire and motivate you as you listen for God's message in your own life!
>
> (cloth) ISBN 1892016117 **$18.95**

Since Life Isn't a Game, These Are God's Rules
Kathy Collard Miller

Subtitled: *Finding Joy & Fulfillment in God's Ten Commandments*

Life is often referred to as a game, but God didn't create us because he was short on game pieces. To succeed in life, you'll need to know God's rules. In this book, Kathy Collard Miller explains the meaning of each of the Ten Commandments with fresh application for today. Each chapter includes scripture and quotes from some of our most beloved Christian authors including Billy Graham, Patsy Clairmont, Liz Curtis Higgs, and more! Sure to renew your understanding of God's rules.

(cloth) ISBN 189201615X   **$17.95**

God Things Come in Small Packages
Susan Duke, LeAnn Weiss, Caron Loveless, and Judith Carden

Subtitled: *Celebrating the Little Things in Life*

Touching reminders of God's simple but generous gifts for us all come to life in this beautiful hardcover gift book with two-color interior. Best-selling writer, LeAnn Weiss combines her signature personalized Scripture with heartwarming vignettes and reflections by Susan Duke, Caron Loveless, and Judith Carden.

(hardcover) 1-892016-28-1   **$12.95**

God Things Come in Small Packages for Moms
Susan Duke, LeAnn Weiss, Caron Loveless, and Judith Carden

Subtitled: *Rejoicing in the Simple Pleasures of Motherhood*

God's special gifts for mothers are bought to life in this beautiful hardcover gift book with two-color interior. Best-selling writer, LeAnn Weiss combines her signature personalized Scripture with stories sure to refresh, uplift and encourage mothers.

(hard cover) 1-892016-29-1   **$12.95**

Seasons of a Woman's Heart
Edited by Lynn D. Morrissey

Subtitled: *A Daybook of Stories and Inspiration*

A woman's heart is complex. This daybook of stories, quotes, scriptures, and daily reflections will inspire and refresh. Christian women share their heartfelt thoughts on Seasons of Faith, Growth, Guidance, Nurturing, and Victory. Including Christian women's writers such as Kay Arthur, Emilie Barnes, Luci Swindoll, Jill Briscoe, Florence Littauer, and Gigi Graham Tchividjian.

(cloth) ISBN 1892016036   **$18.95**

Treasures of a Woman's Heart
Edited by Lynn D. Morrissey

Subtitled: *A Daybook of Stories and Inspiration*

Join the best-selling editor of *Seasons of a Woman's Heart* in this touching sequel where she unlocks the treasures of women and glorifies God with scripture, reflection, and a compilation of stories. Explore heartfelt living with vignettes by Kay Arthur, Emilie Barnes, Claire Cloninger, and more.

(cloth) 1-892016-25-7 **$18.95**

If I Only Knew . . . What Would Jesus Do? for Women
Joan Hake Robie

Subtitled: *Over 100 Ways to "Walk the Walk" and "Talk the Talk"*

Finally a *WWJD?* just for women! Today's woman is faced with more life choices and decisions than ever before. The author follows up on her successful book, *If I Only Knew . . . WWJD?* with a look at the lives of today's women. Get the right perspective—Jesus' perspective—for the day-to-day aspects and challenges of life.

(trade paper) ISBN 1892016087 **$9.95**

The *God's Word for the Biblically-Inept™* series is already a best-seller with over 100,000 books sold! Designed to make reading the Bible easy, educational, and fun! This series of verse-by-verse Bible studies, topical studies, and overviews mixes scholarly information from experts with helpful icons, illustrations, sidebars, and time lines. It's the Bible made easy!

The Bible—God's Word for the Biblically-Inept™
Larry Richards

An excellent book to start learning the entire Bible. Get the basics or the in-depth information you are seeking with this user-friendly overview. From Creation to Christ to the Millennium, learning the Bible has never been easier.

(trade paper) ISBN 0914984551 **$16.95**

Revelation—God's Word for the Biblically-Inept™
Daymond R. Duck

End-time Bible Prophecy expert Daymond R. Duck leads us verse by verse through one of the Bible's most confusing books. Follow the experts as they forge their way through the captivating prophecies of Revelation!

(trade paper) ISBN 0914984985 **$16.95**

Health & Nutrition—God's Word for the Biblically-Inept™
Kathleen O'Bannon Baldinger

The Bible is full of God's rules for good health! Baldinger reveals scientific evidence that proves the diet and health principles outlined in the Bible are the best for total health. Learn about the Bible Diet, the food pyramid, and fruits and vegetables from the Bible! Experts include: Pamela Smith, Julian Whitaker, Kenneth Cooper, and T. D. Jakes.

(trade paper) ISBN 0914984055 **$16.95**

Women of the Bible—God's Word for the Biblically-Inept™
Kathy Collard Miller

Finally, a Bible perspective just for women! Gain valuable insight from the successes and struggles of such women as Eve, Esther, Mary, Sarah, and Rebekah. Interesting icons like "Get Close to God," "Build Your Spirit," and "Grow Your Marriage" will make it easy to incorporate God's Word into your daily life.

(trade paper) ISBN 0914984063 **$16.95**

Life of Christ—God's Word for the Biblically-Inept™
Robert C. Girard

Girard takes the reader on an easy-to-understand journey through the gospels of Matthew, Mark, Luke, and John tracing the story of Jesus' life on earth. Icons, illustrations, chapter overviews, study questions, and more make learning about the Virgin Birth, Jesus' miracles and parables, the Crucifixion, and the Resurrection easier than ever. Over 100,000 sold in this series!

(trade paper) ISBN 1892016230 **$16.95**

Romans—God's Word for the Biblically-Inept™
Gib Martin

The best-selling *God's Word for Biblically-Inept™* series continues to grow! With over 150,000 copies sold, this series is proven to make learning the Bible easy, educational, and fun. Learn about the Apostle Paul, living a righteous life, and more with help from graphics, icons, and chapter summaries.

(paperback) ISBN 1-892016-27-3 **$16.95**

The **What's in the Bible for . . .**™ series is designed to help readers at various stages of life gain biblical insight for contemporary living. From mothers to teens and couples, each title in this series will be an invaluable source of guidance and encouragement as readers *Learn the Word*™ through Scripture, bullets, icons, definitions, chapter summaries, and more. From the makers of the *God's Word for the Biblically-Inept*™ series.

What's in the Bible for . . .™ Women
Georgia Curtis Ling

What does the Bible have to say to women? Women of all ages will find biblical insight on topics that are meaningful to them in six simple sections including Faith, Family, Friends, Fellowship, Freedom, and Femininity. This book uses illustrations, bullet points, chapter summaries, and icons to make understanding God's Word easier than ever!

(trade paper) ISBN 1-892016-11-7 **$16.95**

What's in the Bible for . . .™ Mothers
Judy Bodmer

This second release of the *What's in the Bible for . . .*™ series uses biblical wisdom to help moms cope with life's demands. Icons, illustrations, chapter summaries, and more make understanding God's plan easier than ever!

(trade paper) 1-892016-26-5 **$16.95**

The Weekly Feeder
Cori Kirkpatrick

Subtitled: *A Revolutionary Shopping, Cooking, and Meal-Planning System*

The Weekly Feeder is a revolutionary meal-planning system that will make preparing home-cooked dinners more convenient than ever. At the beginning of each week, simply choose one of the eight preplanned weekly menus, tear out the corresponding grocery list, do your shopping, and whip up a great meal in less than 45 minutes! The author's household management tips, equipment checklists, and nutrition information make this system a must for any busy family. Included with every recipe is a personal anecdote from the author emphasizing the importance of good food, a healthy family, and a well-balanced life.

(trade paper) ISBN 1892016095 **$16.95**

More God's Abundance
Compiled by Kathy Collard Miller

Subtitled: *Joyful Devotions for Every Season*

Editor Kathy Collard Miller responds to the tremendous success of *God's Abundance* with a fresh collection of stories based on God's Word for a simpler life. Includes stories from our most beloved Christian writers such as Liz Curtis Higgs and Patsy Clairmont that are combined ideas, tips, quotes, and scripture.

(cloth) ISBN 1892016133   **$19.95**

God's Abundance for Women
Compiled by Kathy Collard Miller

Subtitled: *Devotions for a More Meaningful Life*

Following the success of *God's Abundance*, this book will touch women of all ages as they seek a more meaningful life. Essays from our most beloved Christian authors exemplify how to gain the abundant life that Jesus promised through trusting Him to fulfill our every need. Each story is enhanced with Scripture, quotes, and practical tips providing brief, yet deeply spiritual, reading.

(cloth) ISBN 1892016141   **$19.95**

Stories of God's Abundance for a More Joyful Life
Compiled by Kathy Collard Miller

Like its successful predecessor, *God's Abundance* (100,000 sold), this book is filled with beautiful, inspirational, real-life stories. Those telling their stories of God share scriptures and insights that readers can apply to their daily lives. Renew your faith in life's small miracles and challenge yourself to allow God to lead the way as you find the source of abundant living for all your relationships.

(trade paper) ISBN 1892016060   **$12.95**

God's Unexpected Blessings
Edited by Kathy Collard Miller

Subtitled: *What to Expect When You Least Expect It*

Over 50,000 sold! Learn to see the unexpected blessings in life. These individual essays describe experiences that seem negative on the surface but are something God has used for good in our lives or to benefit others. Witness God at work in our lives. Learn to trust God in action. Realize that we always have a choice to learn and benefit from these experiences by letting God prove His promise of turning all things for our good.

(cloth) ISBN 0914984071   **$18.95**

Eat for the Health of It
Martha A. Erickson

Subtitled: *Better Nutrition for a Better You*

A back-to-basics approach to eating and maintaining your body. Tells why some people gain weight easily and how to improve your health with or without medicine. Gives 21 reasons why blood cholesterol rises. Includes anecdotes, meal plans, recipes and resources. *Eat for the Health of It* will have you eating towards a better life.

(trade paper) ISBN 0914984780 **$15.95**

Allergy Cooking With Ease
Nicolette M. Dumke

Subtitled: *The No Wheat, Milk, Eggs, Corn, Soy, Yeast, Sugar, Grain, and Gluten Cookbook*

A book designed to provide a wide variety of recipes to meet many different dietary and social needs, and whenever possible, save you time in food preparation. Includes recipes for foods that food allergy patients think they will never eat again, as well as timesaving tricks and an Allergen Avoidance index.

(trade paper) ISBN 091498442X **$14.95**

The World's Oldest Health Plan
Kathleen O'Bannon Baldinger

Subtitled: *Health, Nutrition and Healing from the Bible*

Offers a complete health plan for body, mind and spirit, just as Jesus did. It includes programs for diet, exercise and mental health. Contains foods and recipes to lower cholesterol and blood pressure, improve the immune system and other bodily functions, reduce stress, reduce or cure constipation, eliminate insomnia, reduce forgetfulness, confusion and anger, increase circulation and thinking ability, eliminate "yeast" problems, improve digestion, and much more.

(trade paper) ISBN 0914984578 **$14.95**

Migraine
Charles Theisler

Subtitled: *Winning the Fight of Your Life*

This book describes the hurt, loneliness, and difficulty that migraine sufferers live with. It explains the different types of migraines and their symptoms, as well as the related health hazards. Gives 200 ways to help fight off migraines and shows how to have fewer headaches, reduces their duration, and decrease the pain involved.

(trade paper) ISBN 0914984632 **$10.95**

God's Vitamin "C" for the Spirit™
Kathy Collard Miller & D. Larry Miller

Subtitled: *"Tug-at-the-Heart" Stories to Fortify and Enrich Your Life*

Includes inspiring stories and anecdotes that emphasize Christian ideals and values by Barbara Johnson, Billy Graham, Nancy L. Dorner, and many other well-known Christian speakers and writers. Topics include: Love, Family Life, Faith and Trust, Prayer, and God's Guidance.

(trade paper) ISBN 0914984837 **$12.95**

God's Vitamin "C" for the Spirit™ of Women
Kathy Collard Miller

Subtitled: *"Tug-at-the-Heart" stories to Inspire and Delight Your Spirit*

A beautiful treasury of timeless stories, quotes, and poetry designed by and for women. Well-known Christian women like Liz Curtis Higgs, Patsy Clairmont, Naomi Rhode, and Elisabeth Elliott share from their hearts on subjects like Marriage, Motherhood, Christian Living, Faith, and Friendship.

(trade paper) ISBN 0914984934 **$12.95**

Purchasing Information:

www.starburstpublishers.com

Books are available from your favorite bookstore, either from current stock or special order. To assist bookstore in locating your selection be sure to give title, author, and ISBN #. If unable to purchase from the bookstore you may order direct from STARBURST PUBLISHERS. When ordering enclose full payment plus shipping and handling as follows: Post Office (4th Class)—$3.00 (Up to $20.00), $4.00 ($20.01-$50.00), 8% ($50.01 and Up); UPS—$4.50 (Up to $20.00), $6.00 ($20.01-$50.00), 12% ($50.01 and Up); Canada—$5.00 (Up to $35.00), 15% ($35.01 and Up); Overseas (Surface)—$5.00 (Up to $25.00), 20% ($25.01 and Up). Payment in U.S. Funds only. Please allow two to three weeks minimum (longer overseas) for delivery. Make checks payable to and mail to: STARBURST PUBLISHERS, P.O. BOX 4123, LANCASTER, PA 17604. Credit card orders may also be placed by calling 1-800-441-1456 (credit card orders only), Mon-Fri, 8:30 a.m. to 5:30 p.m. Eastern Standard Time. Prices subject to change without notice. Catalog available for a 9 x 12 self-addressed envelope with 4 first-class stamps.